MIKADO
MEMORIES

MIKADO MEMORIES

Richard Suart

For Cath and Jonny,

remembering Susan and Chris

Foreword

'Well, I'm going to get rid of all that campy Japanese nonsense for a start' – and thus Jonathan Miller lured Eric Idle into playing Ko-Ko in his production of *The Mikado* for English National Opera way back in July 1986. 'I'm not having any of those silly knitting-needles-in-the-hair rubbish.' 'The audience should feel as they come out of this show that they have over-eaten an enormous cream meringue.'

Indeed, audiences have been pouring out of this iconic production for over 200 performances spread over 33 years; it may be in black and white, but there is nothing dated in its staging or ability to entertain.

I want to remember many of those whose talents have contributed to its success, and of course we have to start with Jonathan, who was at the height of his creative powers in the eighties.

He had already created a hugely popular *Rigoletto*, set in New York, and Peter Jonas, Lord Harewood's successor at ENO, was desperately trying to find a production that would help replace the shortfall in government funding, thus helping the company to survive.

Jonathan provided the answer. He must have been aware of G. K. Chesterton's observation, 'I doubt if there is a single joke in the piece that fits the Japanese. But all the jokes in the piece fit the English, if they would put on the cap.' And Chesterton continues: 'The great creation of the play is Pooh-Bah. I have never heard, I do not believe, that the combination of inconsistent functions is specially a vice of the extreme East. I should guess the contrary; I should guess that the East tends to split into steady and inherited trades or castes; so that the torturer is always the torturer and the priest a priest. But about England Pooh-Bah is something more than a satire; he is the truth. It is true of British politics (probably not of Japanese) that we meet the same man twenty times as twenty different officials. There is a quarrel between a landlord, Lord Jones, and a railway

Opposite: Jonathan Miller in rehearsals

company presided over by Lord Smith. Strong comments are made on the case by a newspaper (owned by Lord Brown), and after infinite litigation, it is sent up to the House of Lords, that is Lords Jones, Smith and Brown. Generally the characters are more mixed. The landlord cannot live by land, but does live as a director of the railway. The railway lord is so rich that he buys up the newspaper. The general result can be expressed only in two syllables (to be uttered with the utmost energy of the lungs): Pooh-Bah.'

You can see how all this appealed to Jonathan's sense of humour. From his early days in Footlights he loved poking fun, and he would always convince his cast that *The Mikado* was as English as Buckingham Palace garden parties or the Eton-Harrow match. He wanted them to play it as English panto, which he described as a series of acts strung together on a thread by a highly implausible story. Yet the feeling was to be one 'of the Ascot scene in *My Fair Lady*, or Saturday morning at the Food Hall in Harrods.' The television programme *A Source of Innocent Merriment* chronicled some of the rehearsal period, including moments of uncontrollable mirth as Jonathan writhes around the floor in ecstasy at Eric Idle's idea of kissing the Mikado's boots and licking their soles by way of appeasing him for having killed the heir to the throne. Anthony Van Laast, the choreographer, remembers the rehearsal period as one of utter entertainment from Jonathan, interspersed with him making funny noises, which he delighted in.

The concept was Jonathan's, but he surrounded himself with a magnificently talented creative team who translated his ideas into reality. Jonathan was The Great Entertainer, and also editor; he gave free range to his colleagues, thus empowering them to contribute, which had the positive effect of making everyone feel that they were a necessary ingredient in this exciting project. The atmosphere he created in a rehearsal was a positive force for good in which others could thrive. It is a gift beyond rubies.

Another insult, and, I think, a light one!

Opposite: Frances McCafferty and chorus

THERE COMES A TIME in any company's existence that financial constraints lead to some of the most inventive and creative solutions – and the birth of this *Mikado* was certainly one such. Peter Jonas, who had recently arrived as General Manager of ENO, discovered in his second year that the beginning of his new 1986/87 season could not be realised because there were insufficient funds. He knew that Jonathan Miller was keeping a space free as he was hoping to begin a Rossini series over a period of years, but this too had to be postponed. What was necessary was a new production that would be an obvious hit with the public. He had recently borrowed Jonathan's production of *The Magic Flute* from Scottish Opera to save costs, and shortly after that production opened at the Coliseum, the two met for supper in Camden. There Peter Jonas put to Jonathan the idea of a new production of *The Mikado*. It turned out that this was a popular suggestion, and very soon afterwards he came up with this very engaging and witty staging that reflected just what *The Mikado* is really about. Working on a single set, which would save money, the production gradually fell into place. Sue Blane was engaged as costume designer and Stefan Lazaridis as set designer.

Jonathan and Stefan had been working together in Florence earlier in the year on a new *Tosca* and so had had time to discuss the set for *The Mikado*. It was a piece of genius that Stefan was engaged by Peter Jonas because of course he had no pre-conceived ideas about the piece, being an Ethiopianborn expatriate Greek. His formative years had nothing to do with the precious world of Gilbert and Sullivan, and so he approached the brief with a clear mind. This was essential to Jonathan's concept of a 1920s setting, based on Marx Brothers movies, in particular *Duck Soup*. He wanted Stefan to do *The Mikado* as a show, which is not the way he usually worked.

I will let Alison Nalder, Stefan's assistant at the time, describe more fully the creative process:

It was vital to get the basics right, and the set design is central to the success of any show because it informs the production. It can be very restrictive, and clearly in this case it could not be: there had to be space for cast,

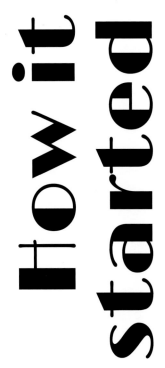

How it started

Opposite: Ian Caddy, Richard Suart, Eric Shilling with dancers

chorus and dancers – the latter were to be significant in the show's success, though no one could have imagined it at this stage.

The Mikado was first premiered in 1885 by the D'Oyly Carte company. It was re-designed in 1926 and the production had remained essentially the same until 1982, when the company was wound up. *Mikado* had become a fossil, with its blocking and stage 'business' set in stone. However, it was now 1985; the operetta was out of copyright and ripe for a new approach.

As a designer Stefan was a notable contrarian – if a director came to him with an idea, Stefan couldn't resist going in the opposite direction. He hated to be told and would do battle with the director until – eventually – some agreement was forged.

Stefan Lazaridis

I worked as Stefan's assistant on and off for about ten years. He was a great stage designer but he was emphatically not a model maker and seldom even sketched what he visualised. Instead he used his assistant as an extension of himself – a sort of amanuensis. On his instructions, the scenic model would be mocked up and then altered repeatedly until he was satisfied.

Stefan and Jonathan decided to set *Mikado* in an English hotel in the 1920s. Like all models, this one started out constructed of white card, but unlike most, it remained white. Dislocated tall white walls encrusted with neo-classical detail and areas of exposed brickwork, with a white floor of giant parquet. But on closer examination there were clearly surreal motifs apparent: white spheres suspended randomly, chairs and musical instruments emerging from the wall, a giant phonograph horn.

Model of the set by Alison Nalder, now in the V&A

The overall effect of Stefan's set design was one of mysterious beauty. However this impression was short-lived – the wit and vigour of Jonathan's production soon took over: the Marx brothers inspiration, the frenetic dance numbers choreographed by Anthony Van Laast and the witty black-and-white costumes designed by Sue Blane.

Opposite: Robert Murray with David Stout and chorus

Above and opposite: photographs of the set model, showing different lighting

The built set as lit for 'Alone, and yet alive'

A few years previously Stefan had worked with David Pountney on *Rusalka*. Stefan had a surreal, dream-like setting, also predominantly white in colour. When we were working on the *Mikado*, elements of the *Rusalka* design crept into the model – the giant nursery fireplace, the crescent moon. This was no accident. Stefan had decided to see himself as an 'auteur' in the cinematic sense, so he rather self-consciously ensured that design motifs reoccurred from one production to the next in order that they would be recognised as his 'signature'.

In Michael Romain's excellent book, *A Profile of Jonathan Miller,* he interviews Stefan, who tells of his enjoyment of watching Marx Brothers movies with the director.

I tried all sorts of ideas for the designs with Busby Berkeley and big Hollywood extravaganzas, and then I hit upon Syrie Maugham, the 1930s decorator par excellence who 'invented' white-upon-white-upon-white. When we were sitting in the Anglo American (in Florence), Jonathan pointed out some sculptural details in the plasterwork and said 'Maybe we should explore the architecture in a rather bizarre way because of the illogicality of the piece.'

We cannot attribute the design solely to the hotel where they happened to be sitting at the time, because a space was needed where people could come and go, scenes could take place, and another follow seamlessly. With the bedrooms at the back, it allows for an almost Feydeauesque farce, much the same as the Brian Rix ones that I grew up with. Having designed them in, Stefan insisted that Jonathan use them, which he does of course, a little naughtily, in the Act 2 Madrigal, when the bell-hops and maids can be seen delivering towels, watering plants and being lured into Ko-Ko's bedroom. The bedrooms were also used to great effect in the final scene when Katisha hauls her new husband up there for a Finale of passion. Stefan sums it up in Michael Romain's book:

> It's such a bizarre piece that the Emperor of Japan and the English Hotel came together quite effortlessly – the series of illogicalities upon illogicalities simply took off. We even put a view of Mount Fuji behind the window as an in-joke (have you ever spotted it?). It's a nonsense piece and we reflected this with all sorts of things – decapitated heads, references to Margaret Dumont and Carol Channing, and so on. I enjoyed it all very much – it is a sizzling show, staged with great panache and bubbling spirits.

'Girls/Kimonos' 2

'Schoolgirls' 2

SueBlane

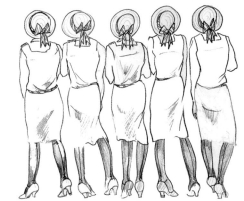

MIKADO

'Schoolgirls' 1

SueBlane

SUE BLANE, THE COSTUME DESIGNER, had already been contracted by Peter Jonas. She never really understood why, but I think we can put it down to the fact that, like Stefan Lazaridis, she had had nothing to do with Gilbert and Sullivan before: she had no prior knowledge, no baggage. Her list of stage credits was already illustrious, particularly after her huge success with *The Rocky Horror Show* in 1972, just a year after graduating from the Central School of Art and Design. The idea of using predominantly blacks and greys against Stefan's white-upon-white was inspired, and her beautiful designs are another key element in the success of this show. I thank her for allowing me to use some of her drawings here. This was her first time with English National Opera and also working with Jonathan and Stefan which made her understandably nervous. She would go on to work with Stefan on many more occasions and developed a great respect and love for the man who, despite being a tough taskmaster, was a huge inspiration and fount of knowledge, and she remembers a joyous time in the creative process.

'Katisha' MIKADO
SueBlane

Right from the beginning it was put to Sue that the production was going to be strongly influenced by Marx Brothers movies, which meant black and white of course, in a totally white set. She was thrilled:

> It was manna from heaven to me. At the beginning of a production period for a designer, all that she has are her drawings, what is important is what happens to them – how the costumes are created from the drawings, and that is the fun part. You begin then to have something concrete, something that you can hold or wear – then there is life.

She actually designed the Gentlemen of Japan first; she cannot remember why, but it was with them that she went to her first technical meeting with Jonathan and Stefan and they were delighted. From that moment onwards there was no looking back. I asked her about the headless dancers that appear in Act 1. She designed them 'with some difficulty actually' and the wonderful ENO prop-costume department gave

'The Mikado'
SueBlane

MIKADO · 'Bellhops'

MIKADO · 'Chambermaids' SueBlane

YUM-YUM WEDDING.

them life, as indeed they did with the Mikado's fat suit. This came from a suggestion from Jonathan, who relished Richard Angas's height and considered that some extra girth would be a bonus —as he remarked, 'we might as well make him as broad as he is tall'. Sue duly obliged and it is a costume of genius. She remembers some nervousness when fitting the girls in the chorus with their school uniforms 'because nobody likes school uniforms – well men do perhaps...!', but it all worked out well especially when they were introduced to their glorious white wedding dresses. The men were easier as Jonathan had given them all individual character – Diaghilev and the like – so Sue had something fun to work on. In dressing the dancers Sue remembers the immense help given by Anthony Van Laast and his assistant Suzanne Hywel. It was clearly a wonderful collaborative process and there seemed to be a great chemistry between them all. I suggested she must have had great fun going out to find samples of different materials in black and grey and all combinations of the two, but, as she pointed out, in those days there were plenty of people employed by the opera companies: cutters, makers, dyers and printers and the like whose job it was to go in search of these. At the end of the day they would all meet up back at Lilian Baylis House, and with a bottle of wine, discuss what they had found that day, what could be used and perhaps what might not, what would work together. 'It's a long process.'

MIKADO   'Gentlemen of Japan' 1
SueBlane

MEN'S CHORUS
'Gentlemen of Japan'   ACT I

Looking back, Sue sums it up by saying what an absolute pleasure it was to be collaborating with Jonathan and Stefan. 'Two such extraordinary people. Over the years I have spent a lot of time with them each individually, with Stefan in Bayreuth, and all three of us worked together at La Scala on *La Fanciulla del West,* which was quite an adventure, but not always a happy one because La Scala were playing funny tricks.' She recalls spending a lot of time with Jonathan in Florence rehearsing *Così fan tutte* – they would dine together each night and Jonathan would ask her to choose a topic of conversation, then off he would go giving her a Miller Masterclass in whatever she had chosen. 'It was extraordinary, always witty, always enjoyable and just magic.'

A KEY PART OF THE CREATIVE TEAM is of course the conductor, and in 1986 the opening shows were under the baton of ENO's Assistant Music Director, Peter Robinson, who had worked with Jonathan earlier in the year on a TV presentation of *Così fan tutte* for the BBC. Peter tells the wonderful story of his actually not being Peter Jonas's first choice conductor. The latter confided in him that he had originally asked Carlos Kleiber, but he was, understandably, otherwise engaged. This is not as unrealistic an idea as it might seem at first reading, as Kleiber had often let it be known that he really thought *The Mikado* to be a wonderful piece. The request also underlines a story that comes from Covent Garden circles. Carlos Kleiber had just been conducting there, and during a first night party was asked by a member of the Board what he would like to conduct there next, to which the answer came 'Why, *The Mikado* of course!' This somewhat caught the questioner off guard and he was heard to reply, 'Herr Kleiber, you will conduct *The Mikado* here over my dead body.'

Peter knew that he was conducting the show at the beginning of 1986 and was responsible for getting a cast in place. However, the key role of Ko-Ko was difficult to fill, with many hopefuls from the acting world rejected, until of course Eric Idle came along quite late in the day. Peter tells of the decision to let him have singing lessons with the then company teacher Joe Veasey, as they were concerned about balance with the singers in the cast. After a couple of sessions it was agreed by all parties that Eric would just continue as he had always done and it would be fine; and indeed it was.

When it came to the 'Little List' song, curiously enough Jonathan thought that it should just be sung as writ, i.e. original Gilbert, until Eric took Peter to one side one day and suggested that he update it... and the rest, one might say, is history.

One of Peter Robinson's great heroes was Charles Mackerras, who had a wonderfully catholic taste in music, which ranged from Handel to Janáček, and from Mozart to Sullivan and well beyond. His versatility was truly amazing, but the secret of his success was in the preparation – respect a piece and give it care – which is exactly how Peter rehearsed *The Mikado*. He knew that Jonathan, although he could not read music, was a great respecter of it, and he never went against where the music was leading. A good working relationship between conductor and director in the rehearsal room is vital

Eric Idle

Opposite: Richard Suart

to the success of a collaboration, and the results speak for themselves.

As a postscript to his Kleiber story, Peter tells of the time when, a few years later, he was rehearsing a gala at ENO and was just about to conduct Eric Shilling singing the Nightmare Song from *Iolanthe*, when he glanced up at the Royal Box and thought that he saw a familiar figure sitting with Peter Jonas. Probably half way through the Lord Chancellor, he realised that it was Carlos Kleiber. Was he here to listen to him conducting Sullivan? Alas in likelihood not, as the next item in the programme was Jane Eaglen singing the Liebestod, conducted by Reggie Goodall. Peter has the refreshing attribute of being a delightfully modest conductor!

As a footnote to the above, I should add that Gilbert & Sullivan has subsequently been performed at The Royal Opera House. Welsh National Opera's production of *The Yeomen of the Guard* enjoyed three performances during one of their annual residences, and I gave my Jack Point. As we gathered in the auditorium for the afternoon balance test, Charles Mackerras began by rehearsing the overture. After the first chord, he stopped the orchestra to announce: 'There, that is the first sound of Sullivan's music ever to grace this House – except of course for my very own *Pineapple Poll*!'. It was a sell-out.

THE FINAL INGREDIENT of this extraordinary creative team was the choreographer, Anthony Van Laast, but this was an inspired appointment. Anthony had been a pupil at Tonbridge School, but shortly before leaving, he was taken to see Nureyev dance at Covent Garden, and his career direction changed overnight from becoming a doctor to a dancer. He studied at London School for Contemporary Dance, and joined the school's associate company in 1971. He left them in 1979 to pursue a freelance career as choreographer and teacher. David Ritch, Jonathan's Associate Director, had seen Anthony's work on *Bluebell,* the BBC series about a nightclub dancer, and suggested to Jonathan that the two should meet. They got on well, and Anthony's services were secured.

Keith Jameson and Sarah Tynan

Opposite: Mary Bevan

Anthony Van Laast and Jonathan Miller

This was a piece of brilliant luck because Anthony instantly understood what was required of him. 'I always had to come to work in the morning full of ideas, this is what Jonathan expected: we would try them and he would take what he liked; we were contributors, and he the editor.' Twelve dancers were hired: some were friends of Anthony's from the West End, including the wonderful Suzanne Hywel who also worked as his assistant, and others were part of the movement group that worked regularly at ENO. They included the ever-youthful Carol Grant who had begun her career with London Festival Ballet, and who is now Head of Movement at ENO and thus responsible for rehearsing the dancers in *The Mikado*.

Anthony's career has been spectacular, from *MAMMA MIA!* (2001) to *Beauty and the Beast* (2017), and from *Annie Get Your Gun* (1986, the year of *The Mikado*) to *Bombay Dreams* (2004). I also had the good fortune to be choreographed by him at ENO in *The Merry Widow* in 2009. He looks back at the rehearsal period and indeed the whole production with much pride. He was a relatively new kid on the block, but Jonathan made him want to do his best, to contribute, because what he would create he knew would last – they all had a good feeling about the whole project.

The dancers all worked for a week before the general rehearsals began, accompanied as ever by the wondrous Elaine Korman. Because of the period, tap dancing was required. Carol was asked at audition, do you tap? Yes of course, she replied, rather diffidently, having been trained in ballet, but learnt how to very quickly!

Anthony tells the story of a stage rehearsal when

Opposite: Dancer strewing petals before the entrance of Ko-Ko

The tap dancing Finale to Act I, from the opening season

suddenly the creative team was summoned to the front of the stalls by the conductor. The tap dancers were making too much noise leaving the stage after their number during quiet music in the following scene. But he never had any trouble solving this kind of problem – which is why you will see the dancers take off their tap shoes disconsolately and leave the stage very quietly and only slightly peeved.

The bulk of the choreography goes to the dancers, but of course the principals and chorus must dance too. The cleverness of Anthony's direction means that, for instance in the Act I Finale, you will think that the whole stage is dancing. In truth, the dancers certainly are, and the principals too to a lesser extent, and the chorus are given key elements of the choreography which they contribute. The result is magnificent.

Opposite: Entrance of bellhops: 'Behold the Lord High Executioner'

Eric Idle and Felicity Palmer

Opposite: Yvonne Howard

I HAVE OF COURSE OMITTED one key person in the creative process and at this point I'll admit to a large gap in my knowledge when it comes to lighting designers, who are in fact crucial to the success of any production. They occasionally come to final studio rehearsals, but after that they are very much in the dark, and here is the problem – they spend hours looking at us when we cannot see them at all. I have met Davy Cunningham, who lit *The Mikado,* only once and that was in Bregenz when we were both using the house computers. Of course it was Davy who recognised me and after he introduced himself, we found we had a lot in common.

He was born and lives in Scotland and has lit well over 250 shows all over the world. He read philosophy at Stirling University and has worked with the finest directors and designers, including of course Jonathan and Stefan on many other shows.

The stage is bright for most of the time – it cannot avoid being – and it is one of the few shows that I have done where the audience is pretty well lit from the bounce-back from the stage – oh yes, we can see you as well! There are some stunning effects too, particularly for Katisha in Act II.

THERE IS ONE OTHER PERSON who was absolutely key to the success of *The Mikado* and that was the Associate Director, David Ritch. David was Jonathan's right-hand man and interpreted a lot of what was suggested into what was possible; his contribution cannot be overestimated. For those of you who saw the show between 1988 and 2008, it was David who was responsible for reviving the production and I salute him for the professional way in which this was always achieved.

David had trained as an actor and in 1952 joined the Old Vic Company; as he pointed out to Rodney Mills in an interview for *Opera* magazine in 1999, 'I got my first professional job in Lilian Baylis's theatre, and thirty years later I am still working for her.' After the rigours of rep theatre, he trained to be a teacher in the sixties: 'I loved working with nine- or ten-year-old kids, the age when they explore, when they are ready for anything, when they aren't inhibited, before

puberty, before peer pressure.' Quite by chance he met the opera director John Copley in 1970, who was directing a new *Carmen* for Sadler's Wells in their new home at the Coliseum. Shortly after their first meeting, John rang David to ask him to come and help with the dialogue as the cast were having real problems in the new space. 'It was thrilling working with the singers: they were just like my nine- and ten-year-olds! They had the same trust in me!' The production was a great success; so too the dialogue, which was praised by the critics. Colin Graham then asked David to come and help with a new production of *The Tales of Hoffmann* the following year. Following another success, he was asked to join the company as a staff producer. David was then asked to form a staff producers' group, 'I didn't really know what a staff producers' group was, but thought that if no one else had invented one, I'd better get on and do it.' It eventually became known as the Staff Directors Department and for many years David acted as its Head, and thereafter as Production Associate to the Company. He went around the world restaging ENO productions that had been exported, many of them Jonathan's. The Company could have had no better ambassador.

There is one story that I must include in my appreciation of David which sums up his true professionalism. He had been assisting David Pountney on a new production of *The Makropoulos Case* and had cycled into the theatre to attend the morning dress rehearsal. Asking the House Manager quite casually whether there were many Friends in attending the dress, he was told that yes there were, and that they were eagerly waiting for his performance. David was not aware that Josephine Barstow was ill, and that her cover did not yet know the production. Then David Pountney came over and begged him to walk the rôle 'otherwise we don't have a dress rehearsal'. The old actor came out in David and he decided to go for it. News quickly spread of this historic undertaking. 'By the third act there were more people in the auditorium than at the beginning. They insisted I took a curtain call, and that was the best round of applause I have ever had in this theatre.'

David Ritch

Opposite: Robert Lloyd and chorus

I first met David in 1984 when I joined the company to understudy the rôle of Bunthorne in *Patience*. I was struck immediately by the care that he took with the dialogue: this was my first brush with G&S professionally and I was beginning to learn so much. Every consonant, every vowel, every syllable – they were all needed – just the same energy as singing. The tempo was important too so that the text could be heard in the Coliseum. He knew it all, and he taught it to me. I am eternally grateful.

When New York City Opera borrowed *The Mikado* in 2001 and 2003 I spent many delightful weeks there with him; he introduced me to friends and we met socially constantly. He was such good fun, and the Americans adored him. You see, he really knew what he was doing, he prepared his score, his professionalism was consummate. Many budding directors under his wing went on to do great things, but they all remember with gratitude the grounding that they had with David. Jonathan was fortunate to have such a talented and faithful right-hand man.

He sheds some interesting light on Jonathan too. In an interview for the *Los Angeles Times,* he says quite candidly: 'With Jonathan there is always a team spirit – a great generosity and sharing of ideas. He's not an authoritarian, and because he believes that he cannot do it on his own, everyone gets to feel important.' 'I don't see my relationship with him as a cross to bear, I know my own value. So does he. Someone has to remember the things he's forgotten!'

Alas, David died in 2018, but he is well remembered. As well as admiring his directorial skills, Sue Blane recalled that 'socially he was magic – a wonderful escort'. Yes, and in my opinion, a much undervalued asset of English National Opera.

PETER JONAS WAS ULTIMATELY responsible for the creation of this *Mikado*, because he was the General Manager at the time and it was his idea. But it was up to others to run with this idea, and of course the leader of the pack was Jonathan Miller. It was Jonathan who gathered the team round him, and

Felicity Palmer and Findlay Wilson

Opposite: Claudia Huckle and Fiona Canfield

this sowed the seeds of the success of the production for, as we have seen, he chose wisely.

This was very much his style of direction, though. Jonathan created a wonderful atmosphere in which contributors could work, and he wanted everyone to feel at home, because he knew that this was the way he could get the best from his team. Everyone was made to feel important: he spoke to each and every person in the room, whether cast, stage managers, chorus or technical.

Of course, he liked to tell stories: he is a wonderful raconteur (witness his stunning appearances on Parkinson and other chat shows). This has an extraordinary effect in a rehearsal room: it unites everyone. This is really important because so many disciplines come together to bring you a production.

Some directors are very manipulative; they like to be in charge. Jonathan would prefer all around him to contribute. He is the final arbiter, but we, the performers, must feel free to perform. That he was adored during the rehearsal period is beyond question – that he inspired is also quite apparent. This can all be witnessed in the delightful documentary that Thames TV made of the rehearsal period, *A Source of Innocent Merriment*. Jonathan can be seen offering suggestions to his cast, entertaining them, and also writhing around on the floor in helpless mirth, so delighted with Eric Idle's boot-licking scene. His eloquence is so entertaining – and he delights in provoking to get further humour.

In some of the pre-publicity to opening night, Jonathan promised 'an Entebbe raid' on those who thought that they alone had the right to perform G&S. This provoked a letter to *The Sunday Telegraph* from I. E. Snellgrove of East Grinstead, which in the interests of balance I reproduce here.

Fortunately, the many thousands who have been entertained by this production since 1986, both in this glorious theatre and also on the big and small screen around the world, will not have shared his diffidence.

BEFORE WE INTRODUCE the characters *The Mikado*, I just wanted to mention how the piece itself was perceived nearly a

HAVING made historical nonsense of "Rigoletto," Jonathan Miller has turned his attention to Gilbert and Sullivan's "Mikado." (Magazine Sept. 7). With typical modesty he proclaims: "Let's launch an Entebbe Raid on this work; let's get it out of the hands of the people who have assumed custody of it." He then assumes custody of it himself in no uncertain fashion, promising us a production which will be "chic," "elegant and charming."

Mr Miller admits that the work of the two Savoyards has always been a mystery to him. He never mentions the libretto, whose subtle satire is clearly beyond him, but he does dismiss Sullivan's music as "silly songs." He compares the opera to the Marx brothers' film, "Duck Soup" and rambles on about Jack Buchanan.

With such a catholic approach to the work he should be able to make it as much a mystery to the Coliseum audiences as it is to him. He certainly did with "Rigoletto."

Such clowning and arrogance could be harmless; I for one care little what he does because a work of art is too strong to be destroyed. But we are told that the ENO is desperately short of money. Why pay Miller a salary to make a mess of "The Mikado" when a real professional could have done a proper job?

Finally, remember that when this intellectual snob talks about the people who have custody of "The Mikado" he means the people who like it, the people who stage amateur productions of it.

I. E. SNELLGROVE,
Harvest Hill,
East Grinstead, Sussex.

Opposite: David Stout

hundred years ago by composer and teacher Thomas F. Dun-hill. He was a great fan, but had to fight his corner. In his prefatory note he states:

> In my efforts to vindicate Sullivan from the severe condemnation which has been passed upon so much of his work I have found it necessary to deal vigorously, and even harshly, with the utterances of some of my personal friends.
>
> I hope they will forgive me.
>
> In the case of Dr Ernest Walker, I may perhaps be allowed in justification, to quote a sentence from his own book, *A History of Music in England.*
>
> 'In his official capacity, no critic of literature or art or anything else recognizes the existence of such a thing as personal friendship, past or present; criticism on any other terms is merely a roundabout name for dishonesty.'
>
> I hope that this incontrovertible view may be shared by Mr. Rutland Boughton and others, with whom, in defence of Sullivan, I have not hesitated to cross swords.

Eric Idle and Richard Van Allan

Those not familiar with Thomas F. Dunhill might like to cast their minds back to their ABRSM Piano exams where his pieces still entertain would-be pianists. In 1939 he wrote a charming operetta, *Something in the City,* and his light opera *Tantivy Towers*, with a libretto by A. P. Herbert, premièred in 1931 at the Lyric, Hammersmith, before transferring to The New Theatre for a six-month run. He taught at the Royal College of Music. He greatly admired Sullivan's music and his study in 1928 broke new ground. There had been many biographies, but Dunhill's was the first by a practising musician to analyse the music.

He writes of *The Mikado:*

> It would be difficult for anyone but the dullest literary bookworm or the stodgiest musical pedant to write without enthusiasm of *The Mikado; or, The Town of Titipu*, which was first presented to a public which had been waiting for it with unprecedented eagerness on March 14, 1885. The date may be regarded as a red-letter one in the annals of

Opposite: Donald Maxwell

Felicity Palmer, Bonaventura Bottone, Susan Bullock and Jean Rigby

English dramatic and musical art. It was obvious from the very start that this was a work of historical importance and that in it the two partners revealed a maturity of execution [sic!] which they had not previously so completely demonstrated.

Iolanthe might have been more fanciful and its humour based on a more poetic foundation; *Princess Ida* might make a stronger appeal to educated musicians by reason of its greater intimacy of style and fastidiousness; but *The Mikado* was incomparably more brilliant than either, and showed a continuous vivacity of movement which all the world could recognize and enjoy.

It was indeed not long before a very large portion of the world was engaged in that recognition and enjoyment. Not only was the work hailed with delight in the United States, but the libretto was translated into other languages, and in Germany particularly, *The Mikado* won as ready an acceptance as in the country of its birth.

Clearly German-born Carlos Kleiber had inherited this enthusiasm. And Jonathan Miller brought it into the twentieth century.

THE REHEARSAL ROOM STAGE IS SET. We have met all those who have been preparing for this moment... but now to meet the cast, who have also been preparing their music and their dialogue. Eric Idle recalls:

> One day out of the blue in July 1986 I got a call from Jonathan Miller. Would I be interested in playing Ko-Ko in his forthcoming production of *The Mikado* at English National Opera? I hadn't foreseen becoming a diva. I asked him what on earth he was going to do with it?
>
> 'Well I'm going to get rid of all that campy Japanese nonsense for a start.'
>
> This I had to see. That's like removing the Japanese from sushi.
>
> 'I'm not having any of those silly knitting-needles-in-the-hair rubbish,' he said.

Did I say that I adore Jonathan Miller? Of course, I said yes, and soon we were rehearsing in the freezing rain of a London summer. They made a documentary of this process called *A Source of Innocent Merriment*, and I got to make one of my comic heroes laugh. It's on-screen too. Jonathan rolled about in hysterics when I began to grovel...

I had never actually seen myself as appearing in opera before, but standing onstage at the London Coliseum with the chorus turned toward me expectantly, and the orchestra sitting up and paying attention, I really enjoyed myself. It went over so well that one night a member of the orchestra said to me, 'Tell me, are you Jewish, or are you just very talented...?

Eric was indeed booked late in the day, as rehearsals began on 11th August – the first night was just five weeks away on 18th September.

Richard Van Allan, Jean Rigby, Eric Idle and Richard Angas

Richard Angas was to play the Mikado. A gloriously tall man with a huge and affable character to match, he continued in the rôle for many seasons and gave 156 performances before he died in 2013 – a great loss to his family, friends, colleagues and fans. His widow Rosanne writes:

Richard and I returned from working in opera houses in Germany because Jeremy Caulton invited him to join ENO under the famous triumvirate of Peter Jonas, Mark Elder and notably David Pountney, who was to become his champion and valued friend.

At first, he sang the serious bass repertoire, but presumably Jonathan Miller must have seen another side to him when he asked him to create the rôle of the Mikado. Richard had sung much G&S as a young man locally and in family circles in his home town of Ashtead, Surrey, and was delighted to take on this rôle professionally, particularly in Jonathan's conception. He was in those days (besides being 6'6") rather slim, and the costume weighed a ton!

I recall that his Mikado performances were always a complete joy to him, even though the dancing in that mighty costume was a challenge. He looked forward to every single one, and relished his pre-performance discussions with Richard Suart on the suitability/aptness of Ko-Ko's witty lines on the events of the day for the List Song. These discussions were for him an intrinsic part of the performance.

Indeed, they were for me too, and I miss him deeply.

Another Company singer, Dennis Wicks, also sang the rôle – he had been a member of the Covent Garden ensemble before joining ENO in the seventies in time to sing Hunding in the Goodall *Ring*, and the Grand Inquisitor in *Don Carlos*; he also took part in the first British performances of Henze's *The Bassarids* and the premiere of Iain Hamilton's *The Royal Hunt of the Sun*.

Alfred Marks, the actor and comedian, sang fourteen performances too. A few years before he had sung Wilfred Shadbolt in *The Yeomen of the Guard* for TV, and was a regular

The Mikado

Opposite: Richard Angas

'A more humane Mikado never did in Japan exist'

guest on *The Good Old Days,* so he was a good choice when the management were still of the opinion that you needed a name to sell the show – indeed he sang well, but felt that the large suit was beneath him.

Mark Richardson has also sung the Mikado when he was free from giving either his Pooh-Bah or Pish-Tush, and most recently Robert Lloyd has assumed the rôle for thirteen performances – this great British Bass is no stranger to G&S audiences having given his Private Willis at ENO in the seventies, a rôle which he repeated in San Francisco some years ago when I was out there singing the Lord Chancellor.

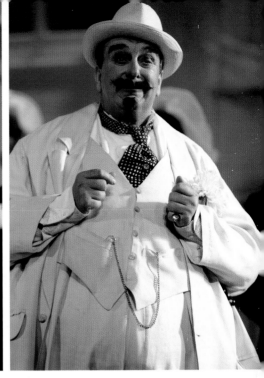

'And I'm his daughter-in-law elect!'

Opposite top: Dennis Wicks

This page top: Mark Richardson

This page and opposite, below: Richard Angas

45 MIKADO MEMORIES

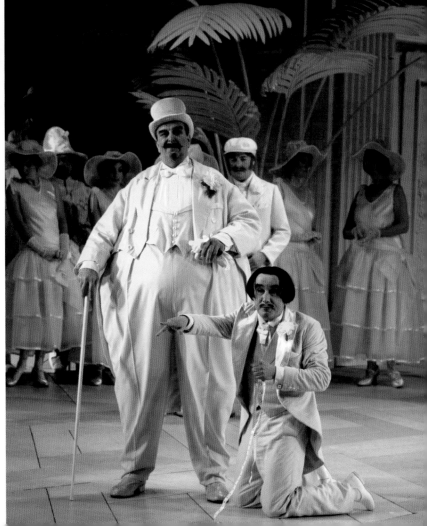

It was an inspired piece of casting to get Eric to play Ko-Ko – and his artistic contribution cannot be overestimated. Anthony van Laast includes him in the creative team, though in the spirit of Jonathan's directing, everyone was encouraged to contribute. But Eric understood where the production was going and was able to draw not only on his huge comedic experience, but also his knowledge of those legendary comedians who had gone before him.

After its success in the 1986/87 season, the company brought the production back for the 1988/89 season, but Eric was unable to return. Convinced that they still needed a name to sell the show, Casting then began to try to find a replacement and eventually came up with Bill Oddie, now known to us principally as an ornithologist (yes, I put him on my list – too easy!), but in those days he was a member of The Goodies too, together with Tim Brooke-Taylor and Graeme Garden. He was a fine television performer but found it difficult to project in such a large theatre as the Coliseum: I had understudied Eric in the first season and was asked to continue this arrangement, even though at the time they had not found anyone for me to cover! Actors are traditionally booked much later than singers as they do not like to commit to a long period with just the odd show per week. Like Eric, Bill was cast quite late in the day, and by that time had committed himself to a family holiday in America over the Christmas and New Year period. I was allowed five performances while he was away, and by good fortune, one of them was on a change of cast day, and so it was reviewed. I have since sung over 150 performances at the Coliseum, plus nearly twenty in New York and a handful in Venice. My good friend Eric Roberts has also given nine performance. He and I were cast as the two pattermen when the New D'Oyly Carte was formed in 1988; he sang Jack Point and I gave my Lord Chancellor.

I am often asked how I keep enjoying Ko-Ko – friends suggest that after so many performances one could get stale and bored. I am afraid that it is just not possible, and every season there are new playmates who bring their own ideas to

Opposite: Eric Idle

'The matter shall have my careful consideration.'

the production. And then there is 'The List', but that is discussed at length elsewhere!

A performer has to be disciplined, and what I remember above all else is that for many in the audience it will be their first visit, or if not, it will certainly be their only attendance during the run. And one also never knows who will be in the audience...

In the eighties, I had also been a member of David Freeman's Opera Factory, and had given performances of Peter Maxwell Davies's *Eight Songs for a Mad King* in the Queen Elizabeth Hall, staged and later televised. I then began to give performances at festivals round Europe and quite often the *Eight Songs* would be paired with Ligeti's *Aventures* and *Nouvelles Aventures*. Ligeti would often be invited, but the downside for him was that he would often have to sit through yet another version of the *Eight Songs* before he got to his own music. However, we did get to know each other. Then one morning in the early nineties I got a telephone call from his agent telling me that Ligeti had attended the performance of *The Mikado* the night before and loved it – would I be in his next opera? Of course I would! Thus I made my debut at the Salzburg Festival in his *Le Grand Macabre* as the Black Minister, a production that also went to the Châtelet in Paris, and would have been the second opera into the refurbished Covent Garden, but the stage machinery did not work in time.

Opposite, top: Eric Roberts; other pictures Richard Suart

Now I'm mentioning all this to illustrate the fact that you never know who will be in your audience, and what might happen subsequently. Ligeti was a composer of immense breadth and interest, and he loved G&S! As a sequel to all this I should mention that I was contacted by a doctoral student in musicology at Stanford University in 2017. He was working on a dissertation that focused on musical settings of Lewis Carroll's *Alice* books. The first half of his study was to be devoted to Ligeti's interest in Carroll, including his sketches for an unfinished *Alice in Wonderland* opera.

My correspondent Joe Cadagin continues:

In the spring, I spent a month researching at the archives of the Paul Sacher Stiftung in Basel, which houses the majority of Ligeti's sketches. In his sketches for the *Alice* opera, he has listed your name as a possible singer, along with Sybille Ehlert and the King's Singers. It seems as if he intended to have you play the White Rabbit and the Mad Hatter, as well as some of the female rôles, including the Duchess.

Can you remember if Ligeti or anyone representing him happened to contact you about this *Alice* project? I would be so grateful for any information you could give me.

This project was actually a commission from ENO, though I found it hard to find anyone there who would admit to that. Ligeti had mentioned it to me, but alas he died before it was ever completed – however he had written a sketch that Joe had found:

Below: Bill Oddie; other pictures Richard Suart

'Close thing that, for here he comes!'

You have the distinct honour of appearing on the back of this musical sketch. On the other side of the paper, Ligeti has written some notes, including (in Hungarian): 'When the Rabbit (Richard Suart) appears, [the music] passes into accelerating chromaticism; suddenly dark/sombre, chromatic.' In total, you're listed ten times in the sketches, mostly, as I mentioned, in possible cast lists, and always in the rôle of the Mad Hatter and the White Rabbit.

Ko-Ko can take you places!

Top right: Eric Idle; other pictures Richard Suart

Lesley Garrett was the first Yum-Yum. It was an ideal rôle for her and came at just the right time in her career. She had already had some notable successes with the Company but this would stretch her and offer her challenges. The dialogue was one of them. A Yorkshire lass through and through, she would now have to adapt to Jonathan's insistence on cut-glass vowels. He wanted her to be 'the heppiest gel in Japan'.

Lesley writes:

Taking part in Jonathan Miller's legendary, mad version of the *Mikado* was one of the most joyous and inspiring experiences of my life. It was like being in the most wonderfully eccentric masterclass... for weeks!

Most days were just hilarious from start to finish – filled with dazzling, creative comedy, diamond-sharp wit and gasp-inducing timing. All of this had to be matched by impeccably stylish singing and elegant, witty playing. Not easy when your diaphragm is impossibly stiff and aching from suppressed laughter.

Occasionally, the frisson of comic genius was elusive and the music refused to cooperate. I vividly remember sharing a pre-rehearsal cuppa with Eric Idle one morning. Stretching my neck and attempting a small arpeggio over PG Tips I announced 'I think I'm going to sing really well today, Eric.' 'Are you?' he replied, quick as you like, 'Well I think I'm going to be really funny, so we should have a good day!'

And we did!

Lesley gave over thirty performances and she never looked back.

The rôle has been an extraordinary starting point for many of ENO's favourite sopranos, and certainly the next one to assume the mantle demonstrates this well: Susan Bullock, who shared the rôle with Lesley in the first season, singing Peep-Bo on her evenings off.

Sue writes:

I remember the very first day of rehearsal in 1986 and the talk through with Jonathan when he said that there wasn't

Opposite: Lesley Garrett

going to be anything Japanese in it whatsoever, and that he was sure that there would be furious letters pouring in to the ENO as a result. Emails hadn't been invented then! We were all rather in awe of Eric Idle and I remember saying to him that I was quite nervous about trying to be funny in front of him... to which he replied 'You are nervous? I have got to try to sing in front of you guys!!' And from that moment on we were all one big happy family.

We sat and watched *Brief Encounter* with Jonathan and he advised us to watch it on a regular basis, paying particular attention to Celia Johnson's accent... 'happy' immediately became 'heppy' for example. I can still quote virtually every word of that film even now.

Ant Van Laast was a very glitzy choreographer, and dance was to be a big part of the production. I remember being terrified at the first dance call. A kinder and more patient man however you could not wish to meet, and I actually enjoyed the dancing element enormously.

My biggest memory of the rehearsal period was laughter... endless laughter. Jonathan creasing up and falling on the floor, helpless with laughter at something that Eric did, Felicity Palmer bashing poor Findlay Wilson to kingdom come, yelling 'Stop that' when he was fussing around her as Katisha's side kick, and then Findlay revealing his Liszt style hair as he took off his flying hat and shook out his long locks and accompanied her on the piano.

Eric crawling on the floor and licking Richard Angas's boots.

The first time we heard the 'Little List'.

I had tears of mirth rolling down my face for several months.

Heaven!

Opposite, top: Sophie Bevan; below: Mary Bevan
This page, top: Lesley Garrett; below: Jeni Bern

'Oh it's quite usual, I think. Eh, Lord Chamberlain?'

And what did I learn?

Comic timing... how to wait a split second longer and get double the laugh for example.

And how much fun a real 'team production' can be.

The opening night was incredible... I still remember the anticipation... and the moment of silence as the music ended before the place erupted.

'Heppy, heppy days' indeed.

I am a great believer in the assertion that singing Gilbert and Sullivan teaches singers how to sing in English really well: it is not easy, and should be taught more at our music colleges. (Here writes a man who is now hired from time to time as Diction Coach.) Energising the spoken word also helps and both of these Yum-Yums are great examples of this – this experience has informed their subsequent marvellous careers.

Another case in point is the third assumer of the rôle, Janis Kelly, who sang over forty performances. She recalls:

My triplet girls were seven in 2001 and had seen many performances and dress rehearsals. They used to enjoy practising the kissing duet between Yum-Yum and Nanki-Poo at home: one would sit on the sofa being me, and another would be the son of His Majesty the Mikado, then following through on a loop continually changing rôle as they went to the back of the queue! It was hysterically funny, and one day we were allowed to go on stage before a show and let them play out their little scene. I had previously done a very traditional production, straight out of college, but this was to be very different and on a very raked stage. I knew Richard Suart from our Opera Factory days, and we relished the eccentricities of our rôles, playing a real world – for, however funny it was, it was never sent up or parodied. Entering on the high wooden floor stage

Opposite, top: Sarah Tynan
Opposite, below left: Rosemary Joshua; right: Jeni Bern
This page, top: Janis Kelly; below: Susan Bullock

'Being engaged to Ko-Ko, you know.'

and running down the hill always made me shriek with laughter – scary and fun. David Ritch helped me speak in the very posh 1920s English accent – I learnt how to keep my natural inflection whilst maintaining a clipped RP black-and-white-television voice. I was also coached by the extraordinary Nina Finburgh whose talent was to help you draw out truth, no matter what accent you have to do.

It is an essential part of my performance practice to this day.

Another favourite ENO soprano whose glittering career included Yum-Yum was Rosemary Joshua, who sang twenty performances. She was followed by Sally Harrison, Alison Roddy, and Jeni Bern, who all made their mark. Sarah Tynan sang twenty performances, Sophie Bevan nine, and her sister Mary twenty-five.

An amazing array of talent who have had impressive careers – Lesley, Sue and Janis recently coming together in *Jack the Ripper: The Women of Whitechapel*.

This page, top: Rosemary Joshua; below, left Jeni Bern; below right: Mary Bevan
Opposite, top left: Sarah Tynan; top right: Sophie Bevan

*'Oh b****r the flowers that bloom in the Spring!'*

Bonaventura Bottone created Jonathan's Wandering Minstrel. He writes:

I have very fond memories of the days spent in LBH participating in the most vibrant production process. Jonathan Miller was so convincing in his presentation that he appeared to have planned every step before we set a foot on the floor in the rôles. The concept was clear, the façade of japonaiserie was to be removed and applied in exquisite touches as an affectation. The comedic effect was sheer delight for us as performers. It allowed us to use the deftest of touches to play Gilbert's text. The tradition of Dame Bridget D'Oyly Carte was, to the aficionados of Gilbert and Sullivan, the only way to play their works. Therefore we were stepping out of a tradition into uncharted audience reaction. I remember Dame Felicity in rehearsal saying, 'I am sure my mother and father will disown me for playing Katisha this way. My parents are players in their local G&S society and the members won't be happy.' Sometime after I had put the trombone down for the 98th time, I rashly asked Uncle Tod, who was then in his nineties, if he had enjoyed the video of Jonathan Miller's *Mikado*. The reply came back in an euphonious Derbyshire tone, 'No lad, I don't like my Gilbert and Sullivan mucked about'. He did later however soften a little towards my performing skills, having seen me at the Buxton Festival play Benda in Dvořák's *The Jacobin*, whereupon he ventured, 'Against my better judgement you were really very good'. In the event, *The Mikado* did polarise opinion, but the ayes had it on the night. The production style had been meticulously crafted upon the English cinematic period of the black-and-white era. Dialogue delivery was based on the traditional English lady and gentleman who remained cool as cucumbers in the most passionate of circumstances. I was asked to play Nanki-Poo as a mixture of Jack Buchanan and Bertie Wooster dressed for the Henley Regatta with a sweet kiss-curl. Around me swirled bellhops and housemaids attending to the gentlemen in the clubroom as I teetered into the scene with my trombone in its case. I watched

Opposite: Bonaventura Bottone

as seasoned singer Richard Van Allan practised twirling his cane around, tossing it skyward and catching it, mostly, in rehearsal. Only once in performance did he miss. His flawless dialogue and dancing I will always treasure. Each gentleman member of the chorus had a character to play and our Findlay had the position of Katisha's chauffeur/accompanist. Findlay found every comedic moment and capitalised on it. Our dialogues tumbled over each other, so cues were vital. Lesley Garrett and I rehearsed every nuanced word in our scenes over and over to ensure a naïvety that was credible. Then we practised our dancing with balletic precision, each foot extension was to mirror the other's. Eric Idle brought his unmistakable voice to his rôle of Ko-Ko. He assumed both a common and a cut-glass accent for effect. It was exciting to be gathered up in the process of bringing so many skills into the performing arena to produce this meringue of such light confection and yet a substantial craftwork. The Three Maids – Lesley, Susan Bullock and Jean Rigby – surrounded by the ladies of the chorus playing every schoolgirl you have ever known, tirelessly rehearsed hysterical giggles and brought brilliant humour to the floor of the room. We laughed – no, we wept – as Eric slithered across the floor for the first time to lick the boots of the Mikado, his falsehood uncovered and his execution cauldron definitely being heated up off stage. Richard Angas, soon to be puffed up like a barrage balloon in his incredible

'You very imperfect ablutioner!'

This page, from top to bottom: Alfie Boe, Bonaventura Bottone, Robert Murray

Oppoiste, clockwise from top: Anthony Gregory, Robert Murray, Barry Banks, Bonaventura Bottone

costume, brought an immense form and genial character to the rôle of the Mikado with the least likely genetic characteristics to be the father of the Heir Apparent. It was a riot of humour to be in the company of the wonderful minds brought together in the rehearsal room. On stage it was a blistering blast of pure joy. Aided and abetted by the sublime choreographer Anthony Van Laast, Jonathan Miller mirrored the true eccentricities of our British way of life viewed through the prism of Gilbert's brilliant text and Sullivan's memorable music.

Bon sang over ninety performances. His children too grew up with the show, and it was a delight to me when I did a new production for Scottish Opera and the D'Oyly Carte in 2015 that his daughter Rebecca was singing Yum-Yum.

Stuart Kale, a company principal in the eighties sang four performances, and Harry Nicholl sixteen. Barry Banks delighted us for over thirty performances before leaving for America. Curiously enough, the next second trombone was the American Keith Jameson who had sung it for New York City Opera when the production was borrowed in 2003. Rob Murray sang over twenty performances, Alfie Boe nine and Anthony Gregory thirteen.

As we saw with our Yum-Yums, all these gifted tenors have continued to have successful careers

This page, top: Bonaventura Bottone; below, Robert Murray
Opposite, left top and below: Bonaventura Bottone
Opposite, right: Keith Jameson

The late Richard Van Allan was Jonathan's first Lord High Everything Else. The two had worked together very successfully the year before on *Don Giovanni*. Quite what the director had in mind for his Pooh-Bah didn't work for Richard and he tried several characterisations before ending up with a Lieutenant-Commander he used to chat to in the pub. This underlines Jonathan's flexibility: he does not like to impose anything on his performers, but rather let them discover something that they find comfortable. When I had injured a knee during a rehearsal period, he offered alternatives to the grovelling scene which kept me off my knees, and it was a merciful relief. He is popular with singers for this. I think he rather likes our company and will often be seen in the canteen or dressing rooms chatting.

Richard grew up in Derbyshire where his first musical experiences were with the local church choir and then in Gilbert and Sullivan productions at his secondary school. Before his voice broke properly, he took the rôle of Nanki-Poo, which is hard to imagine when we remember his sonorous bass voice. He went on to sing many rôles with English National Opera including Boris Godunov, The Grand Inquisitor and Philip II in *Don Carlos*, Claggart in *Billy Budd* and Don Basilio in *Barber of Seville*. He sang the Don when ENO revived Massenet's *Don Quixote*, in 1994. His acrobatics in the windmill scene, where he is carried off into the flies by one of the sails, drew gasps of delight. He performed regularly with all the major British opera companies and was greatly in demand abroad. The range of his rôles was impressive and in the same year that this *Mikado* opened, he became director of the National Opera Studio, where he reminded his students of 'the fantastic importance of the text'. Anyone wishing to understand this basic requirement only had to go to ENO to hear him perform.

Richard gave over fifty performances but Ian Caddy tops the chart with seventy-two. The great Donald Adams came in for a season too; in fact he was my very first Pooh-Bah, and I shall never forget the volume of sound emanating from that legend as we got to the end of the 'I am so proud'

Opposite: Richard Van Allan

trio in Act 1. I had not rehearsed with him, so was not prepared; but he opted for the high F# and it was too wondrous for words. Donald Maxwell has sung over twenty performances and Graeme Danby thirty. Mark Richardson, who holds the record for characters played in this production, has sung fourteen.

'And Chief Rabbi...'

This page, clockwise from top left: Richard Van Allan, Ian Caddy, Graeme Danby and Donald Maxwell.
Opposite, top: Ian Caddy, bottom, Richard Van Allan

Clockwise from above: Donald Adams, Donald Maxwell, Ian Caddy, Donald Maxwell

Felicity Palmer created the Elderly Lady, in love with Nanki-Poo, though she might have been a little reluctant at first...

She writes:

I have vivid memories of sitting in... possibly... Cecil Sharp House... for a talk-through from Jonathan Miller about the forthcoming rehearsals for his new production of *The Mikado*. I was not overly enthusiastic about the prospect of the production, since it had been a replacement for what would have been *A Masked Ball*. I didn't see Gilbert and Sullivan as a terribly exciting alternative!

What is lodged in my memory is the surprise from all of us assembled when Jonathan took us to his home in Camden to watch *Duck Soup*. He wanted Katisha to be based on Margaret Dumont, which was a quite other proposition from what I had expected.

Rehearsals in Lilian Baylis House were huge fun... as Jonathan added bits and pieces to his concept as we went along. I remember his suggesting that when I sang 'The Hour of sadness is dead and gone', it was to be a sort of Queen Elizabeth Hall poker-faced recital – with my long-haired 'pilot' playing the piano – sung, of course, in our over-exaggerated upper-class accents.

The other abiding memory, apart from getting to know and work with Eric Idle, which added a certain frisson to the whole thing, was Jonathan so loving the idea of Ko-Ko licking the sole of the Mikado's shoe (the late, lamented Richard Angas then), that he regularly rehearsed it and, at times, was seen writhing on the floor in paroxysms of laughter.

I don't remember any other rehearsal period being quite so much fun or having so much laughter. Having set out with reservations about playing a lady with, as I expected, a knitting needle through her wig, I ended up having more fun than I could remember, in wild twenties costumes... with not a kimono in sight! Sadly, I had another production that I had to do and left half-way through the run of performances. I was never so sad to leave a production.

Katisha

Opposite: Felicity Palmer

'But I think he will give it better whole than in pieces.'

In all, Felicity only did eighteen performances, but her replacement, Ann Howard, went on to give over fifty.

Ann had come to opera singing after being a West End shop assistant and also touring in pantomime. She rose swiftly via the Covent Garden chorus to dominate the rôle of Carmen for ENO over many years, a rôle which she also sang with Domingo in New Orleans and New York. Other rôles for ENO included Fricka, Hélène in *War and Peace*, Azucena in *Il Trovatore* and Jezibaba in *Rusalka*. By her own admission she liked to play 'witches and bitches' and the daughter-in-law elect was ideal. She was a first-rate performer and indeed my first Katisha, who expected great things of me; she was a most generous colleague and one of those very fine performers that ENO could turn to, having nurtured them so well in their early years. Late in her career we performed *HMS Pinafore* together in New York and relished an early screening of *Forrest Gump*.

Sarah Walker also did a season. We had worked together in Kent Opera on *King Priam* and it was wonderful to welcome her back to the Coliseum some years after her memorable *Gloriana*.

Linda Hibberd also sang the rôle and then came the wonderful Anne Collins who gave nearly forty performances. She was a proper contralto who specialised in character rôles. After training at the Royal College of Music she joined Sadler's Wells Opera, as it then was, in its second year at the Coliseum, singing the Governess in Tchaikovsky's *The Queen of Spades*. The following year she sang the Fairy Queen in *Iolanthe* for the Company, opposite the Private Willis of Robert Lloyd, who returned forty years later to sing the Mikado. She sang in the very first ENO *Ring* cycle under Reginald Goodall in 1973 singing in all four parts: as Erda in *The Rhinegold* and *Siegfried*, Rossweisse in *The Valkyrie* and the Second Norn in *The Twilight of the Gods*. At that time she took on the rôle of the cello-playing Lady Jane in *Patience*, which delighted audiences for

'I have a left shoulder-blade that is a miracle of loveliness. People come miles to see it. My right elbow has a fascination that few can resist.'

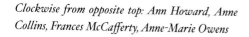

Clockwise from opposite top: Ann Howard, Anne Collins, Frances McCafferty, Anne-Marie Owens

many seasons. It was a very witty production which was later and inexplicably sold to Australian Opera. At Covent Garden she sang many rôles, including Auntie in *Peter Grimes,* and created the rôle of the Angel of Death in James MacMillan's *Inés de Castro* for Scottish Opera. Her obituary in *The Guardian* written by Patrick O'Connor says,

> In later years, she several times returned to ENO as Katisha, seeming to bring some sense to all the antics. Her singing and acting were all the more funny, as she was obviously taking it all very seriously.

But that is the secret of comedy – discipline. She was a truly amazing colleague, no nonsense: she wouldn't do matinees, take it or leave it, and all of us always took it.

Giving almost as many performances over three seasons was the wondrous Frances McCafferty, whom Jonathan encouraged to give her Katisha with a discreet Morningside accent – another example of his willingness to be flexible. We had first met at a concert in Edinburgh where she did indeed appear as Katisha with her knitting needles, which took Barry Banks and me by surprise – she was magnificent, and we were helpless. We subsequently became very good friends and both worked in the D'Oyly Carte together. I was saddened when she was no longer asked to sing Katisha.

Anne-Marie Owens joined us for a season, and Deborah Hawksley and Gaynor Keeble also donned the pearls – tremendous sports all of them.

Most recently Yvonne Howard has been tangoing with me and this has been a delight.

Opposite, clockwise from top left: Sarah Walker, Frances McCafferty,
Yvonne Howard, Frances McCafferty, Ann Howard, Anne Collins
This page: Felicity Palmer

Peep-Bo

Sue Bullock was the original Peep-Bo, whilst understudying Yum-Yum, and this practice continued for a while. Maria Bovino, Claire Daniels, Helen Kucharek, Mary Plazas and Sally Harrison all did seasons and Jean Trevelyan gave two performances. Anne Gerbic managed two seasons before disappearing back to New Zealand, and since then the rôle has been in the safe hands of Fiona Canfield, from the chorus, who has given ninety performances

Pitti-Sing

Jean Rigby sang Pitti-Sing in the first season. She writes:

How lucky was I to be involved in two Jonathan Miller productions.

I had already taken part in *Rigoletto*, his innovative and award-winning production set in 1950's Mafia America. Now I was one of the little maids in *The Mikado*. An added bonus was the other school maids were two of my music college peers, Lesley Garett and Susan Bullock!

From the first day we knew we were on to a winner, there was a permanent buzz surrounding the rehearsal period. No kimonos, a St. Trinian's-style look, a link to *Brief Encounter*, through the very posh-sounding dialogue and Anthony Van Laast as choreographer. To crown everything Lesley, Sue and I would be modelled on Rita Hayworth, Jean Harlow and Louise Brook − what is not to like! The cherry on top would be casting Eric Idle as Ko-Ko; what a stroke of genius and what a comedic talent.

Rehearsals, as one can imagine, were hilarious, I have never laughed so much. There were shades of Cambridge Footlights with Miller and Idle. I remember one rehearsal where Jonathan was talking and the subject matter alighted on, of all things, 'bulldogs balls...'. He ended prostrate on the floor in absolute hysterics. To this day I have no idea what it was about but joined in the hilarity.

During one of the many revivals I was expecting and

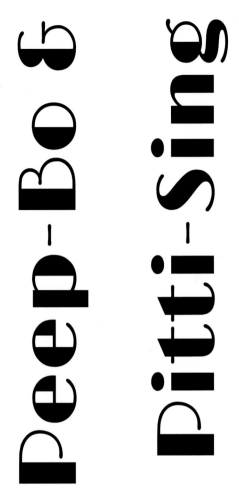

Opposite: Jean Rigby (centre) and Susan Bullock (right) with Lesley Garrett as Yum-Yum

This page: Fiona Canfield and Victoria Simmonds with Jeni Bern as Yum-Yum

given a padded suit to help hide my growing bump. My line 'Won't have to wait very long they say...!' added a much greater meaning than usual. During a subsequent revival I had to leave the production before the end of the run and Eric gave me a wonderful 1920s print of a flapper, which he signed. I treasure it.

Dr Miller; I thank you for all the wonderful memories.

Jean gave nineteen performances altogether before starting her family, and the very fine company member Ethna Robinson followed in her footsteps. Thora Ker and Elizabeth McCormack did a season each and Christine Botes sang twenty performances. She writes:

It was exciting to be cast as Pitti-Sing in Jonathan Miller's legendary production of *The Mikado* in 1991. Already a G&S groupie, the opportunity to sing a medium-sized rôle in a dazzlingly successful show was almost too good to be true, and I knew we were in for a lot of fun. Yum-Yum was Rosemary Joshua and Peep-Bo was Anne Gerbic. We wore our gymslips with glee and threw ourselves into our schoolgirl rôles. However, I had reckoned without our first entrance. Fans of flat racing will understand when I say that 'Three Little Maids' is opera's equivalent of a two-furlong dash. Over almost before it starts, it can never be quite fast enough. Or so it felt. We were put into strict training by the excellent Jim Holmes and David Ritch.

Above Jean Rigby and Susan Bullock with Lesley Garrett as Yum-Yum
Below left: Julie Gossage. Below right: Anne Marie Gibbons
Opposite: Fiona Canfield and Victoria Simmonds

Hours of rehearsal time were devoted to singing, running, posturing, squealing, eyelid-batting and, above all, diction; so, by the first performance we were in the peak of condition and could take whatever the grown-ups on stage might throw at us. This was just as well since it included threats of marriage, beheadings, being buried alive and similar Gilbertian horrors.

Our reward for all this speed was not in heaven but at the start of Act 2. It was lovely, knowing what an exquisite tableau had been created for the beginning of the scene, to be ready and in position for the placid charm of 'Braid the Raven Hair'.

Pitti-Sing has become a very good testing ground for ENO artists, which is why most of them only do one season, including Julie Gossage, Anne Marie Gibbons, Anna Grevelius and Claudia Huckle, though Nerys Jones, Victoria Simmonds and Rachael Lloyd managed two a-piece. It's a pretty impressive list!

Mark Richardson began his long association with this production creating Pish-Tush with Jonathan, although the early days were not easy as Mark recalls:

> I couldn't buy into the cut-glass accent, and so after two weeks Jonathan suggested a nouveau-riche Northern industrialist, and we went from there; but he did this without hesitation. His productions always allowed for flexibility, and that really marked him out.

Mark started his life at ENO as a member of the chorus, but Colin Graham and Jonathan suggested that he come out and begin doing smaller rôles, 'bits and pieces' as Mark modestly describes them. He points out that this production had only three guest artists, the rest were cast from Company Principals, of which he was one.

> It was very much a team show, a company show – and that gave it a great confidence. We could all chip in and say what we thought, and Jonathan encouraged this. I remember the talk-through at the beginning of the rehearsal period when we were introduced to the set and listened to Jonathan's ideas, some of which seemed a little far out at the time. Sensing a slight unease, he just finished by saying that what he wanted to achieve at the end of the rehearsal period was a great big meringue of pleasure. He wanted to bring delight and to give entertainment.

Mark later played Pooh-Bah and has a wonderful suggestion: 'I don't think that Jonathan was ever really totally happy with anyone who tried their hand at Pooh-Bah, and this is because, deep down, this was the character that he wanted to play himself, though he knew he could never sing it.'

The third rôle he has played is the Mikado in what he describes as 'the hottest costume on earth'. He is full of praise for the way Richard Angas played the character. 'It was very subtle; it was in fact wonderfully underplayed. It takes a lot of courage to come onto a stage three-quarters of the way through a piece, surrounded by dancers and chorus, sing your big number, and still manage to retain that subtlety. It took a long time for me to understand that and appreciate it.'

Opposite: Mark Richardson

This page, left: William Robert Allenby; above: Arwel Huw Morgan

Opposite: clockwise from top left: Riccardo Simonetti, David Stout, George Humphreys, Eric Shilling

Pish-Tush was soon given to Eric Shilling, another Company Principal and he sang it for five seasons and gave seventy-five performances. When I was beginning my career, Eric was already a legend, and so it was an utter privilege to share a stage with him. He had begun his career in 1945 singing Marullo in *Rigoletto* at Sadler's Wells, but it was not until 1959 that he joined the company full-time, singing many of the comic and dramatic character rôles – Jupiter in *Orpheus in the Underworld* and Rostov in *War and Peace*. I remember his Colonel Calverley in *Patience*: impeccable diction, and an inspiration to us all. He was the consummate Company Principal and an absolute gentleman.

Arwel Huw Morgan was another very useful company member who assumed the rôle for four seasons, and then it was handed to Riccardo Simonetti and Toby Stafford-Allen. Those that followed used it as a spring-board for successful careers: Richard Burkhard, William Robert Allenby, David Stout and George Humphreys. An illustrious lot!

'If this is true, it's jolly for you, Your courage screw, to bid us adieu.'

Opposite, top: Richard Burkhard; below, Toby Stafford-Allen. This page,
clockwise from top left: George Humphreys, Eric Shilling; Riccardo Simonetti

The chorus plays a vital part in the success of this show. I asked Judy Douglas, who has been in the chorus for the entire run of the production, and with whom I was at the Royal Academy of Music, to put down a few thoughts:

Where to start with memories of the *Mikado*? So many, so varied, but nearly all happy. Wonderful to have been a part of the original creation of such an iconic production... the surreal experience of walking into the Coli canteen to see the whole of the Monty Python cast sitting around a table...

Something that unfortunately has been lost over the last thirty-three years was the creation of the characters of the gents chorus. I remember that every costume was created to represent an historical character – Glyn Adams was Diaghilev, Gerald Holding was Noël Coward. There was also Rasputin, the villain from Charlie Chaplin movies, W. H. Smith (as the First Lord of the Admiralty) and many more.

One overriding memory, and still relevant to this day, is the pain of wearing high heels on a steeply raked stage: my feet are hurting right now just to think of it!

I have many happy memories of all the ex-choristers, many of whom are now unfortunately no longer with us, some of whom professed to hating G&S but who couldn't help but enjoy themselves once the show had started. Nothing more thrilling and heart-warming than to hear the audience reaction at the end of a show: makes the job worth doing. After 36 years at ENO, the *Mikado* will always be one of my favourite productions and happiest shows.

They sing, they dance, they react. Together with the dancers, they form the heart of the show. Traditionally, Katisha's pianist comes from amongst their ranks. I should give him his full title as it appears in the programme – Katisha's pilot, accompanist and unrequited love. For many years he was played by Findlay Wilson; upon his retirement, he graciously handed the joy-stick to Murray Kimmins, who then handed it on to David Newman.

Chorus

'If you want to know who we are...'

Anyone who has seen this production will acknowledge that the dancers are an integral part of its success and so I just want to write about them briefly. They not only dance their hearts out, but do come across as actual characters, even though they are deprived the privilege of either singing or speaking; they communicate solely with their bodies, and their success is a great achievement.

Anthony and his Assistant Choreographer, Suzanne Hywel, came from the West End. They cleverly knitted together a group of twelve, some of whom joined them from the West End, but others were from the ENO Movement Group such as Carol Grant. Carol's career began with London Festival Ballet and then she became a freelance dancer whose first job with ENO was *A Night in Venice,* when Pauline Grant was Head of Movement in 1973. She would return to the company after a gap of ten years and then was chosen to be one of the dancers in *The Mikado*. Her last shows were in 2000. She is now Head of Movement at ENO and is responsible for auditioning new dancers for the group. She relates that there is a greater turnover of boys, to which I naughtily remarked that this was because they were not visitors to Ko-Ko's bedroom. This refers to the Madrigal in Act 2 when there is a certain amount of coming and going upstage with girls replenishing towels in the guest bedrooms: the boys are taking drinks to guests and there is some plant-watering too (and a little singing too I believe!). Carol was for many years snatched by Ko-Ko into his room whilst clutching a pile of towels; another chambermaid is seen leaving glugging from a bottle of champagne in a rather dishevelled state... Feydeauesque...!

She reminded me of another dancer who was in the first run of performances, Colleen Barsley, who a little later married the wonderful bass Stephen Richardson. In 2015 he and I were both in another production of *The Mikado* for Scottish Opera and the D'Oyly Carte, and although they live in France now, Colleen came over to see a performance in Southamptonn. It was a glorious reunion after nearly thirty years.

Stephen Speed (Speedy) was one of the original boys. He used to carry the NO FLIRTING sign at the beginning of

Dancers

Opposite: Carol Grant

the show, and act very indignant when Nanki-Poo refers to his 'Nancy on his knees'. After his performing days were over Stephen would come and revive the choreography. We spent many happy days in Venice sharing a flat with David Ritch whilst mounting the production there. Alas, neither he nor Suzanne Hywel is with us any more – wonderful memories tinged with great sadness.

Carol Grant has to choose dancers who have had some sort of classical training:

> There's a lot of the choreography that's classical ballet – a lot of the stuff that the bell-boys do has to be very neat and tidy, and that's what I try to make happen when I revive it. I have to drive them really hard. It's got to be exact, otherwise it's messy, and that's no good.

It's down to discipline again.

In the 1988/89 season, when I began performances, Elaine Tyler-Hall joined the dancers. She recalls:

In 1988 I was a jobbing freelance dancer working in London doing lots of different things – film, TV, working in dance companies and dancing in opera. I had worked many times at the Royal Opera House, but never at the Coliseum. Then I heard that there was an audition for *The Mikado*. The wonderful Sue Hywel suggested that I come along, but at the audition I thought that I had no hope of getting the job as I felt so much taller than anyone else in the room! However, somehow I did get it and so began my 31-year (so far!) association with the show.

My experiences with the show have been joyous; I cannot think of a more appropriate word.

Anthony and Sue always chose dancers who had lots of character, and there were some big personalities among the dancers: Carol Grant, Barbara Rhodes, Speedy

(Stephen Speed) and many, many more. Sue, who revived the choreography for all of the early revivals, demanded a lot from the dancers: they must dance accurately with great energy and style, and really perform. She was an expert tapper herself, and she made sure that average tappers like myself really upped our game! But that does not mean that those rehearsals were not some of the most wonderful and enjoyable I ever experienced; we really had fun.

Once we dancers had drilled the choreography in our own studio we joined the main cast and the inimitable David Ritch was in charge. A consummate actor himself, he was rigorous in keeping the production in check and not allowing too much camp to creep in (some, but not too much!). I was always fascinated listening to him rehearse the dialogue scenes, with love and absolute precision.

One of my favourite moments at every show was never seen by the audience. During the overture all the dancers were on stage behind the tabs. Speedy gave a whole solo performance which would have brought the house down. It was both technically brilliant – he was a fabulous dancer – and howlingly funny.

I learned so much from all these wonderful people. This production has been lucky enough to have had some incredible talent connected to it, and it is their contributions that have made it what it is.

As time passed I was dancing less, and assisting, choreographing and directing more. I had always been fascinated by the process of putting an opera together, both artistically and technically, and I loved the challenge of being in the thick of it. I was very lucky to be able to make that shift across the pit and was privileged to assist and work with many really fabulous directors. Of course I missed out on working with Jonathan on *The Mikado* because I only joined the gang for the second season of performances.

But as a staff director at ENO I worked on his *Rigoletto* and at last I did assist him! With Jonathan in the room, rehearsals are a blast – his anecdotes have everyone in stitches. I think he would be the first to admit that he does not enjoy the 'blocking' part of the job (he has blocking anecdotes!), but he is the master of ideas and understanding people. He can resolve the problems of a whole scene by just a few words, and change the performance of a singer by a small suggestion. Genius! And I love to hear him insist that everyone in the company has equal value, from the highest-profile star on the stage to the technicians in every department backstage: they all contribute their time and talent, and every production needs all of them. He is always thrilled to chat to the backstage people, and they adore him – he is a generous and wonderful man. I went on to assist Jonathan on *L'elisir* and a small production of *Carmen*, and finally, once David had retired from reviving Jonathan's

work, came full circle to reviving some of his productions including *The Mikado*.

When I revive *The Mikado* I have some huge shoes to try to fill and I know I never can. But I hope that I have learned some of the magic that these people created, and I try to emulate them and be faithful to their vision.

And that's how important the dancers are – how wonderful that one of them has now risen through the ranks to now revive this iconic production.

Whilst only a handful of singers have been associated with each rôle, the conductors' roster is a long one.

Peter Robinson commenced proceedings and then returned to celebrate the 25th anniversary of the production. Quite often the baton was passed to other members of the music staff – David Drummond, Martin Handley, Jim Holmes, Noel Davies, Justin Brown, Stephen Clarke, Alex Ingram, Murray Hipkin, Martin Fitzpatrick and most recently a Charles Mackerras Fellow, Fergus Macleod.

Sian Edwards is the only Musical Director to have conducted a season. Mark Shanahan, John Pryce-Jones and Gareth Jones I had come across in the D'Oyly Carte, and Simon Lee I used to teach French to when he was a chorister at Ripon Cathedral Choir School before I went to university. David Parry has conducted a season and Wyn Davies two. He writes:

> I was very much a new boy and particularly in awe of Eric Shilling who was singing Pish-Tush, and whom I'd seen over the years but not met before. He was a perfect model of professionalism. Attentive to every detail in what to him must have seemed a diminutive rôle and attentive even to the rookie conductor.
>
> Amongst many pleasures were the chorus who gave every impression of being interested in yet another conductor's approach. And I remember particularly the wind soloists who still delighted in Sullivan's writing.
>
> The *Mikado* was the beginning for me of a friendship with Richard Angas whose graciousness and poise in rehearsal as well as performance are still so much missed.
>
> (And as for whoever was playing Ko-Ko, I thought it unlikely he'd be booked again.)

Michael Rosewell also conducted two seasons – in all, quite a wonderful array of British conductors who have all been entranced by this production. I remember dear Wyn on one occasion being so engrossed in the dialogue on stage that he quite forgot to start the next number.

It has always been important for Ko-Ko to encourage a good rapport with the maestri because somehow we have to

Conductors and orchestra

find our way through the Little List together, and I would like to thank them all for being so attentive and modest in allowing me to dictate the song's progress – there have been some hairy moments but we have always finished together. I have only had cause to put one of them actually on the List, and that was because he decided to scrap the overture. A popular inclusion.

A KEY GROUP OF WONDERFUL MUSICIANS I have yet to name: the ENO Orchestra, who have so patiently and expertly accompanied this production throughout its long journey. I pay tribute to them all for their enthusiasm and encouragement, and above all for their friendship. We meet each other mostly in the canteen where they let me know if they approve of the list's inclusions, and quite often make suggestions of their own.

It is very difficult to get to meet them all, but occasionally one meets them outside the confines of the Coliseum. I was sitting in a bar with friends in Hythe a few years back, when a gentleman approached me and introduced himself as my Second Trombonist. He was Les Lake who had only recently retired from the orchestra after many years' service, now enjoying some freedom down by the coast.

This reminds me of a story concerning a preview of the show in 1986 when, with fifteen minutes to spare, the Orchestral Manager discovered that the second trombone had not arrived. (Remember those days before mobile phones?) Nanki-Poo in his disguise as a second trombonist was otherwise engaged, so the orchestral manager had a brainwave. He popped over to the *Lamb and Flag* in Rose Crescent to ask the landlord, a recently retired player, if he could come and help out. Alas the pub was far too busy for him to get away, but he spotted someone who was able to help. A trombonist had just popped in for a pint after a hard day rehearsing *Phantom of the Opera* at Her Majesty's Theatre. Approached by Richard Smith, the orchestral manager, he looked a bit bemused at first, but readily agreed as he borrowed a dinner jacket and bow tie from Richard whilst running back to the Coliseum. He was paid a bonus for being so willing to help out at such short notice.

Opposite: Anthony Gregory

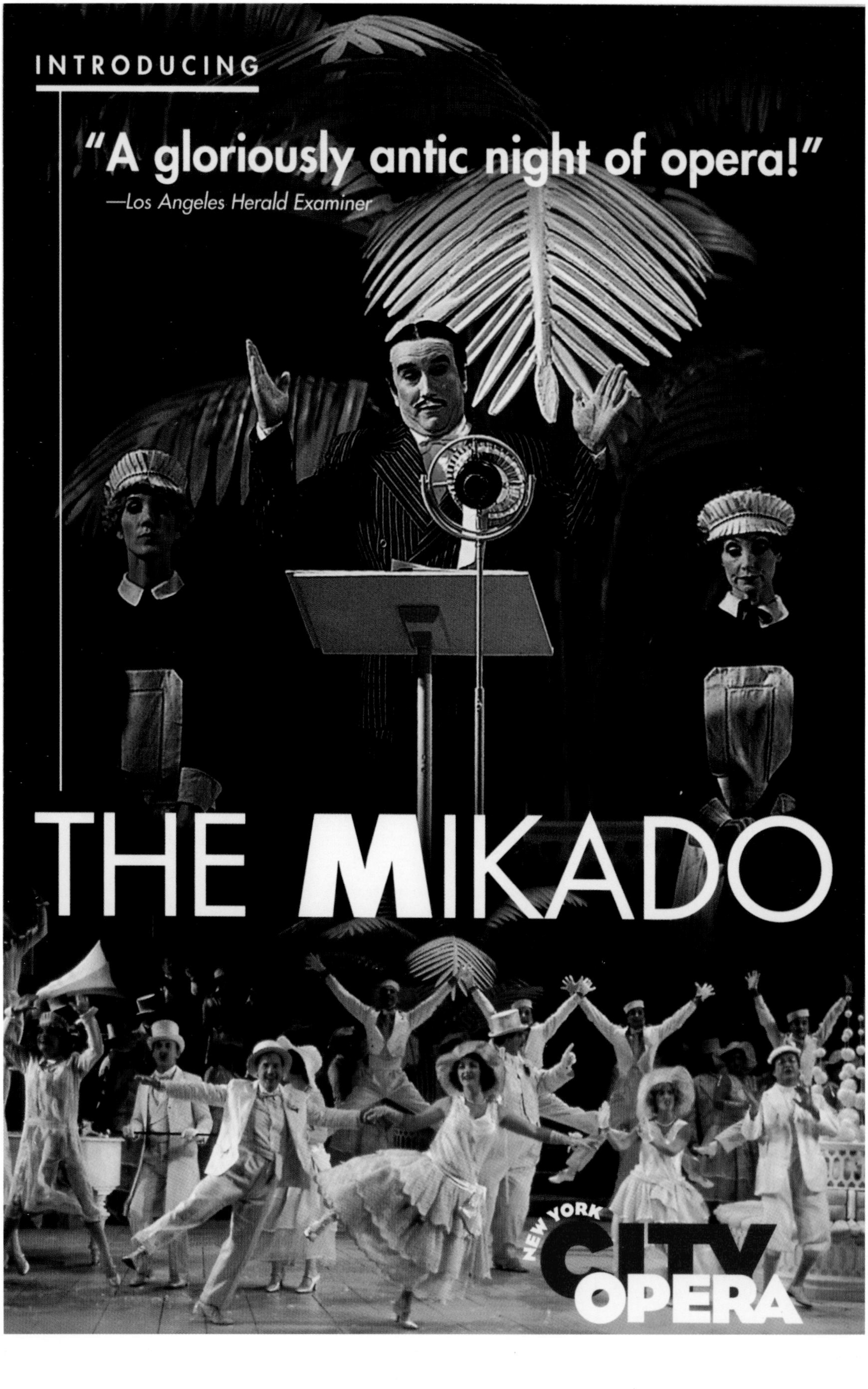

INTRODUCING
"A gloriously antic night of opera!"
—Los Angeles Herald Examiner
THE MIKADO
NEW YORK
CITY
OPERA

There was a fair amount of pre-publicity about this new production, so by the time it came to opening night there were no real surprises, other than the fact that what people had read so much about beforehand they were now going to see unfold before their very eyes – and by and large it went down well.

As a wonderful red herring, ENO let it be known that Dr Miller would not be able to attend the first night as he was going into orbit. The mind boggled – was he so afraid of the G&S aficionados that he felt it necessary to go to such exotic lengths to escape their awesome fury? No, having just passed his fitness tests, he would indeed be flying high over the USA because he was making a TV programme about weightlessness.

The critics were almost unanimous in their praise; indeed, reading them some 33 years later, one is struck by how polite they all were. I recommend a return to this discipline.

Hilary Finch in *The Times* was enthusiastic:

This new production has put the work back where it belongs: on its toes in the brightest footlights of musical theatre.

Any fears that stripping away the Japanese costume would leave Gilbert's satire uncomfortably naked... are soon dispelled. By locating this *Mikado* among the wags and the flappers who so enjoyed staging the thing itself, and by reinvigorating the distancing effect of Gilbert's own debunkings, Miller does the trick. What is more, this audacious send-up within a send-up in a world of posing poseurs is animated by some of the most sophisticated timing and adroit routines G&S have probably ever known.

The wonder is that so much falls into place so effortlessly, and, in doing so, has the effect of realigning the ear just at those points where any but the most avid G&S groupie is likely momentarily to switch off.

Christopher Grier in the *Evening Standard* welcomed it too:

The result is a sophisticated period musical, faithfully placed on the familiar notes and words of a still earlier generation. What verbal changes and extras there are sound apposite.

Opposite: Publicity card used by New York City Opera, 2001

Arthur Jacobs, who really knew his Sullivan, wrote in the *TLS*:

> Jonathan Miller has brought off a dazzling and entertaining conjuring-trick. Now you see *The Mikado*, now you don't. Little remains of the original oriental theme... Gilbert had used Japan as an allegorical mask to attack English hypocrisy. Miller seems not so much to be removing the mask as placing another mask (an English one) over it. Sullivan suffers not a whit in the process.
>
> As for what sense it will all make to such of the Coliseum's patrons as are unfamiliar with *The Mikado*, I hesitate to guess. But W. S. Gilbert, when writing his play *Rosencrantz and Guildenstern*, did not feel obliged to consider those who did not know *Hamlet*.

Francis King, writing in *The Sunday Telegraph*, gets it all mixed up, and frets about the lack of internal logic, which we know Jonathan dispensed with some time ago.

> ... thus, when Ko-Ko is handed a letter from the Mikado, he announces to the audience, 'It's in Japanese' – and turns it sideways to read it. The sight-gag is a good one. But when subsequently the Mikado appears, he is, in the person of Richard Angas, an even more elephantine version of Sidney Greenstreet, in white suit and fedora. Why should he have been writing in Japanese?

But there is redemption:

> The best way to enjoy the evening is to put all these inconsistences, and the exasperation that they cause, out of one's mind, and to concentrate on the witty inventiveness of Miller's direction, the elegance of the set and of Sue Blane's costumes, Anthony Van Laast's fizzing choreography for pert waitresses and dinky bellboys, and a revelation of Sullivan's score in a limpidity too often clouded in the past by clumsy re-orchestration and inadequate playing.

Alan Blyth writing in the *Daily Telegraph* was slightly more enthusiastic than his piece in *Opera* magazine, though neither really welcomed the production:

Practically nothing was left to chance or spontaneity in this highly drilled, relentless, frenetic assault on our laugh buds. 'We're being very funny; you must laugh at us' seemed the clue to the show.

The 'list' was predictably but rather obviously and vulgarly updated, and its intimacy, the idea of Ko-Ko taking the audience into his confidence, was quite lost by having it delivered as a speech to the microphone: this was typical of the whole staging in throwing in an idea without really thinking it through.

Whether Richard Angas, in outsize, off-duty gangster dress was supposed to be Oliver Hardy, Dr Miller himself, or some generalised figure of slightly sinister authority, was unclear. This again was indicative of the satire's lack of focus.

One further word: great play was made by the producer and the programme of taking the Marx Brothers as an inspiration. Their great gift was to make their farcical antics seem entirely natural and spontaneous. Here, fatally, the actors seem to be insisting on telling us how funny and witty they were being. For me, that immediately kills the smile on the face. Very modified rapture.

He cheers up two years later though...

The ENO's riotous but disciplined 1920s *Mikado* in Jonathan Miller's staging has returned... indeed the production now seems... genuinely funny.

Let us allow David Gillard, writing in the *Daily Mail* to have the last word:

It is a measure of Miller's success that Mr Idle – whose vocal prowess is rather unfairly assessed in the programme biography as 'ranging between messy-soprano and bass-Charrington' – fits as snugly into this Jack Buchanan world as ENO's classy singers and, indeed, G&S themselves.

I doubt if even the most conservative Savoyard could take offence at this riotous and splendidly sung piece of Old England. It had me howling in the aisles. Spiffing.

Cast Lists

1986/87 season

26 performances

The Mikado	Richard Angas
	Dennis Wicks
Nanki-Poo	Bonaventura Bottone
	Stuart Kale
Ko-Ko	Eric Idle
Pooh-Bah	Richard Van Allan
	Ian Caddy
Pish-Tush	Mark Richardson
	Eric Shilling
Yum-Yum	Lesley Garrett
	Susan Bullock
Pitti-Sing	Jean Rigby
	Ethna Robinson
Peep-Bo	Susan Bullock
	Maria Bovino
Katisha	Felicity Palmer
	Ann Howard
Conductor	Peter Robinson
	David Drummond
	Martin Handley

Dancers: Colleen Barsley, Carol Grant, Suzanne Hywel, Sarah Kruger, Barbara Rhodes, Stella Segar, William Bowen, Neil Boyle, David Donegan, Bret Macey, Nigel Nicholson, Stephen Speed

1988/89 season

23 performances

The Mikado	Richard Angas
	Alfred Marks
Nanki-Poo	Bonaventura Bottone
	Harry Nicoll
Ko-Ko	Bill Oddie
	Richard Suart
Pooh-Bah	Donald Adams
	Ian Caddy
Pish-Tush	Eric Shilling
	Arwel Huw Morgan
Yum-Yum	Susan Bullock
	Janis Kelly
Pitti-Sing	Jean Rigby
	Thora Ker
Peep-Bo	Claire Daniels
Katisha	Ann Howard
Katisha's pilot	Findlay Wilson
Conductor	John Pryce-Jones
	Jim Holmes
	Noel Davies

Dancers: Carol Grant, Barbara Rhodes, Lynn
Robertson-Bruce, Nikki Squires, Clair Symonds,
Elaine Tyler-Hall, James Huxtable, Ian Knowles,
Bret Macey, Nigel Nicholson, Colm Seery,
Stephen Speed

1986/87

1988/89

1989/90 season

18 performances

The Mikado	Richard Angas
	Ian Comboy
Nanki-Poo	Barry Banks
	Harry Nicoll
Ko-Ko	Richard Suart
Pooh-Bah	Richard Van Allan
Pish-Tush	Eric Shilling
Yum-Yum	Lesley Garrett
	Janis Kelly
Pitti-Sing	Elizabeth McCormack
	Thora Ker
Peep-Bo	Helen Kucharek
	Jean Trevelyan
Katisha	Sarah Walker
	Linda Hibberd
Katisha's pilot	Findlay Wilson
Conductor	Justin Brown
	Jim Holmes
	Wyn Davies

Dancers: Carol Grant, Barbara Rhodes, Lynn Robertson-Bruce, Nikki Squires, Clair Symonds, Elaine Tyler-Hall, James Huxtable, Ian Knowles, Paulo Lopez, Bret Macey, Nigel Nicholson, Stephen Speed

1991/92 season

20 performances

The Mikado	Richard Angas
Nanki-Poo	Bonaventura Bottone
	Barry Banks
Ko-Ko	Richard Suart
Pooh-Bah	Ian Caddy
	Richard Van Allan
Pish-Tush	Eric Shilling
Yum-Yum	Rosemary Joshua
Pitti-Sing	Christine Botes
Peep-Bo	Anne Gerbic
Katisha	Anne Collins
	Ann Howard
Katisha's pilot	Findlay Wilson
Conductor	Jim Holmes
	Mark Shanahan

Dancers: Colleen Barsley, Carol Grant, Karen Halliday, Lynn Robertson-Bruce, Clair Symonds, Elaine Tyler-Hall, James Huxtable, Paulo Lopez, Michael Mercer, Nigel Nicholson, B. J. Ryan, Stephen Speed

1992/93 season

14 performances

1989/90

The Mikado	Richard Angas
Nanki-Poo	Barry Banks
Ko-Ko	Richard Suart
Pooh-Bah	Mark Richardson
Pish-Tush	Eric Shilling
Yum-Yum	Janis Kelly
Pitti-Sing	Julie Gossage
Peep-Bo	Anne Gerbic
Katisha	Anne Collins Linda Hibberd
Katisha's pilot	Findlay Wilson
Conductor	Michael Rosewell Stephen Clarke

1992/93

Dancers: Carol Grant, Karen Halliday, Louisa McAlpine, Barbara Rhodes, Lynn Robertson-Bruce, Clair Symonds, Elaine Tyler-Hall, David Donegan, James Huxtable, Ian Knowles, Paulo Lopez, Christopher O'Loughlin, B. J. Ryan, Drew Varley

1994/95

1996/67

1997/98

1994/95 season

7 performances

The Mikado	Richard Angas
Nanki-Poo	Bonaventura Bottone
Ko-Ko	Richard Suart
Pooh-Bah	Ian Caddy
Pish-Tush	Arwel Huw Morgan
Yum-Yum	Lesley Garrett
Pitti-Sing	Ethna Robinson
Peep-Bo	Mary Plazas
Katisha	Anne Collins
Katisha's pilot	Findley Wilson
Conductor	Sian Edwards

Dancers: Colleen Barsley, Carol Grant, Louisa McAlpine, Lynn Robertson-Bruce, Stella Segar, Clair Symonds, David Donegan, James Huxtable, Ian Knowles, Paulo Lopez, B. J. Ryan, Colm Seery

1996/97 season

8 performances

The Mikado	Richard Angas
Nanki-Poo	Bonaventura Bottone
Ko-Ko	Richard Suart
Pooh-Bah	Richard Van Allan
Pish-Tush	Arwel Huw Morgan
Yum-Yum	Janis Kelly Sally Harrison
Pitti-Sing	Nerys Jones
Peep-Bo	Sally Harrison Fiona Canfield
Katisha	Ann Howard
Katisha's pilot	Findlay Wilson
Conductor	John Pryce-Jones

Dancers: Carol Grant, Gaby Lewis, Lynn Robertson-Bruce, Clair Symonds, Elaine Tyler-Hall, Melissa Were, Matt Fraser, James Huxtable, Jimmy Jillebo, Paulo Lopez, Ginger Salkin, Colm Seery

1997/98 season

7 performances

The Mikado	Richard Angas Mark Richardson
Nanki-Poo	Bonaventura Bottone
Ko-Ko	Richard Suart
Pooh-Bah	Ian Caddy
Pish-Tush	Arwel Huw Morgan
Yum-Yum	Janis Kelly
Pitti-Sing	Nerys Jones
Peep-Bo	Fiona Canfield
Katisha	Anne Collins
Katisha's pilot	Findlay Wilson
Conductor	Michael Rosewell

Dancers: Carol Grant, Karen Halliday, Gaby Lewis, Lynn Robertson-Bruce, Clair Symonds, Melissa Were, Daniel Crossley, Ben Garner, James Huxtable, Simon Rice, Ginger Salkin, Alexis Thomas

2001/02 season

15 performances

The Mikado	Richard Angas Mark Richardson
Nanki-Poo	Bonaventura Bottone
Ko-Ko	Richard Suart
Pooh-Bah	Graeme Danby Ian Caddy
Pish-Tush	Riccardo Simonetti
Yum-Yum	Alison Roddy
Pitti-Sing	Victoria Simmonds
Peep-Bo	Fiona Canfield
Katisha	Frances McCafferty
Katisha's pilot	Findlay Wilson
Conductor	Mark Shanahan Alex Ingram

Dancers: Lucy Casson, Karen Halliday, Louisa McAlpine, Sophie Reynolds, Hayley Sanderson, Kirsty Tapp, Jason Barden, Chris Crompton, Ben Garner, Thomas Paton, Sandy Rass, Colm Seery

2003/04 season

10 performances

The Mikado	Richard Angas Mark Richardson
Nanki-Poo	Bonaventura Bottone
Ko-Ko	Richard Suart Eric Roberts
Pooh-Bah	Ian Caddy
Pish-Tush	Riccardo Simonetti
Yum-Yum	Jeni Bern
Pitti-Sing	Victoria Simmonds
Peep-Bo	Fiona Canfield
Katisha	Frances McCafferty
Katisha's pilot	Murray Kimmins
Conductor	Gareth Jones

Dancers: Lucy Burns, Lucy Casson, Louisa McAlpine, Sophie Reynolds, Hayley Sanderson, Simon Archer, Rain de Rye Barrett, Kit Dickinson, Gavin Eden, James Huxtable, Leighton Morrison, Craig Turner

2005/06 season

12 performances

The Mikado	Richard Angas
Nanki-Poo	Keith Jameson
Ko-Ko	Richard Suart Eric Roberts
Pooh-Bah	Ian Caddy
Pish-Tush	Toby Stafford-Allen
Yum-Yum	Sarah Tynan Lesley Garrett
Pitti-Sing	Anne Marie Gibbons
Peep-Bo	Fiona Canfield
Katisha	Felicity Palmer
Katisha's pilot	Murray Kimmins
Conductor	Simon Lee Murray Hipkin

Dancers: Lucy Casson, Louisa McAlpine, Corinne Ponton, Sophie Reynolds, Nadia Sadiq, Hayley Sanderson, Richard Curto, Chris Crompton, Matthew Graham, Joseph Leigh, Tim Beaumont, Ben Whitson

2001/02

2003/04

2007/08 season

10 performances

The Mikado	Richard Angas
Nanki-Poo	Robert Murray
Ko-Ko	Richard Suart
Pooh-Bah	Graeme Danby
Pish-Tush	Richard Burkhard
Yum-Yum	Sarah Tynan
Pitti-Sing	Anna Grevelius
Peep-Bo	Fiona Canfield
Katisha	Frances McCafferty
Katisha's pilot	David Newman
Conductor	Wyn Davies Martin Fitzpatrick

Dancers: Lucy Casson, Louisa McAlpine, Corinne Ponton, Sophie Reynolds, Nadia Sadiq, Kirsty Tapp, Davide Camorani, Alex France, Hendrick January, David Klooster, Innis Robertson, Gledis Tase

2010/11 season

9 performances

The Mikado	Richard Angas
Nanki-Poo	Alfie Boe
Ko-Ko	Richard Suart
Pooh-Bah	Donald Maxwell
Pish-Tush	William Robert Allenby
Yum-Yum	Sophie Bevan
Pitti-Sing	Claudia Huckle
Peep-Bo	Fiona Canfield
Katisha	Anne-Marie Owens
Katisha's pilot	David Newman
Conductor	Peter Robinson

Dancers: Lucy Burns, Lucy Casson, Caroline Crawley, Kade Ferraiolo, Louisa McAlpine, Lynn Robertson-Bruce, Nadia Sadiq, James Huxtable, Anthony Kurt-Gabel, David Murley, Colm Seery, Craig Turner

2012/13 season

12 performances

The Mikado	Richard Angas
	Mark Richardson
Nanki-Poo	Robert Murray
	Gareth Huw John
Ko-Ko	Richard Suart
Pooh-Bah	Donald Maxwell
Pish-Tush	David Stout
Yum-Yum	Mary Bevan
Pitti-Sing	Rachael Lloyd
Peep-Bo	Fiona Canfield
Katisha	Yvonne Howard
Katisha's pilot	David Newman
Conductor	David Parry

Dancers: Lucy Burns, Lucy Casson, Heather Craig, Bianca Hopkins, Rebecca Lee, Louisa McAlpine, Lynn Robertson-Bruce, Nadia Sadiq, Rain de Rye Barrett, Davide Camorani, Ben Dixon, Anthony Kurt-Gabel, David Murley, Colm Seery, Craig Turner

2007/08

2010/11

2015-16

2015/16 season
13 performances

The Mikado	Robert Lloyd
Nanki-Poo	Anthony Gregory
Ko-Ko	Richard Suart
Pooh-Bah	Graeme Danby
Pish-Tush	George Humphreys
Yum-Yum	Mary Bevan
Pitti-Sing	Rachael Lloyd
Peep-Bo	Fiona Canfield
Katisha	Yvonne Howard
Katisha's pilot	David Newman
Conductor	Fergus Macleod

Dancers: Lucy Burns, Lucy Casson, Julia Davies, Bianca Hopkins, Louisa McAlpine, Nadia Sadiq, Rain de Rye Barrett, Jamie Bradley, Nick Keegan, Anthony Kurt-Gabel, David Murley, Adam Tench

Acknowledgements

I must first of all thank most sincerely my two principal photographers for this book, Billy Rafferty and Fiona Rich, both of whom have devoted their working lives to ENO, and have very generously given me permission to use their images. Billy joined the company (then Sadler's Wells) in 1962 as a driver, ferrying the company's scenery and costumes all over the country and abroad. He enjoyed the work and developed a love for opera (and for one of their dancers, whom he married). He became transport manager, and at this time developed a love for photography; he had a natural talent for it and was appointed the company's resident photographer. After retirement he continued as a freelance, and photographed at ENO until 2014, when poor eyesight forced him to give up. Fiona Rich joined ENO's chorus in 1986 straight from the Royal Academy of Music and straight into the first rehearsals for the production. She has since sung in every performance. Keen readers will have noted that in 1996 Fiona (Canfield) swapped her black chorus bob for blond curls and has sung 90 performances of Peep-Bo. When not on stage she is passionate about capturing drama with her camera, having learnt much of her photography from Billy.

In my search for more material about Stefanos Lazaridis, I would like to thank Keith Warner who put me in touch with Theodosia Papazikou, who in turn suggested I contact Frank Toshack who told me that Stefan's archive had been passed on to the V&A where it was being digitised. Thanks to all of them and to Keith Lodwick at the Museum for sending me photos of the set box. How wonderful to know that it still exists. I was also alerted by them to the existence of Tim Williams's beautiful book entitled *Stefanos Lazaridis*, and I learnt much from the contributors to this, particularly Peter Jonas.

I should also like to thank Fiammetta Doria who spent a day at the British Library for me in search of early reviews, and also Emma Jenkins who read through my script and offered much advice on my abysmal punctuation. I should also like to thank Gill Rafferty for her kind hospitality during my searches through Billy's huge library.

Thanks to the many who have contributed memories to this book: Lesley Garrett, Bonaventura Bottone, Susan Bullock, Janis Kelly, Rosanne Angas, Felicity Palmer, Jean Rigby, Christine Botes, Wyn Davies, Elaine Tyler-Hall, Alison Nalder and Judy Douglas. Thanks too to those who agreed to meet me, Anthony Van Laast, Peter Robinson and Carol Grant; also Eric Idle who has allowed me to use passages from his sortabiography *Always look on the bright side of life*. Sue Blane and Mark Richardson talked with me on the phone. I am most grateful to Sue for allowing me to use her beautiful costume designs. Sincere thanks to Nicholas Roberts at ENO for his help and encouragement and to my children who have kept me at it; and finally my dear publisher Alexander Fyjis-Walker whose enthusiasm for all things *Mikado* has now given birth to my second book about this amazing production.

First published 2019 by
Pallas Athene (Publishers) Limited
Studio 11A, Archway Studios,
25-27 Bickerton Road,
London N19 5JT

www.pallasathene.co.uk

ISBN 978 1 84368 180 9

Editor: Alexander Fyjis-Walker
Editorial Assistants: Patrick Davies and Joshua Hunter

Photographs by Billy Rafferty or Fiona Rich,
except p. 6 from *A Source of Innocent Merriment*,
courtesy of Fremantle Media,
pp. 16-19 courtesy of Sue Blane,
p. 24 courtesy of Anthony Van Laast
and p. 68, top left, courtesy of Alastair Muir

Printed in England

@Pallasathenebooks
@Pallas_Books
@Pallasathenebooks
@Pallasathene